Quilt & Sewing

Project Journal

Coastal Designs 2021

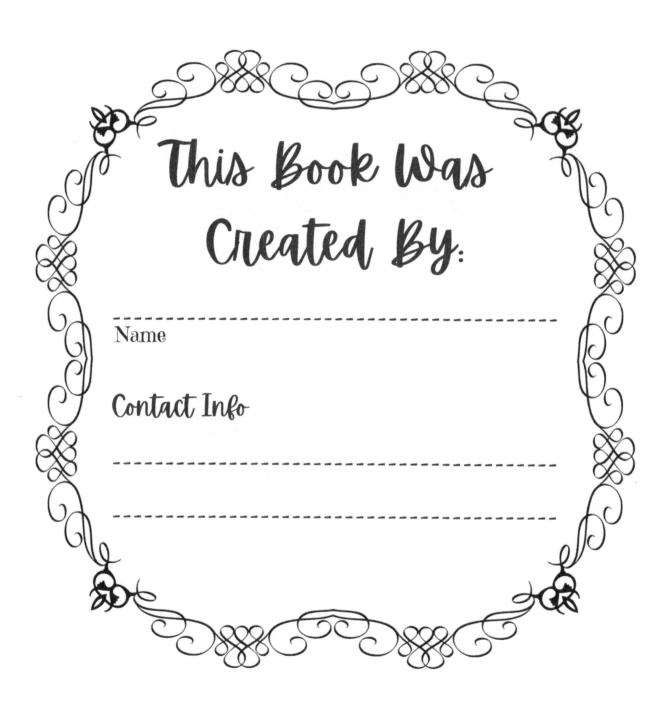

This Book Was Created By:

Name

Contact Info

 # Introduction:

This is a journal for creative souls, to keep track of all your QUILTING and SEWING projects. A place to keep a bit of your crafting history! No matter if you're sewing simple projects or quilts or complex garments, you can keep a record of what and when you made it. This is where you can keep a log of sewing projects you have made, notes on their creation and images or fabric swatches can be attached as well. Keep a record of the process and who has the project now! Use this journal in whatever way suits YOU best!

How to use this Book:

WHAT: Here is where you describe your sewing or quilting project. What is the pattern name and or number? Does the quilt or quilt square have a name? Or give it any name you like! Also keep a record of the finished size here.

WHEN: Keep a record of the date you started, (if you want to) and date of completion.

WHY: Did you make this for a special occasion, a person, an event, yourself? Record that in this section.

HOW: This is where you write Notes about the process. What went wrong and what went right! Were any directions unclear? What did you love about making it? How would you do things differently next time? What thread, fabric, batting, notions, etc. did you use? Where you purchased your fabric and other information goes here.

WHERE: Where is the quilt now? Who has it? Where is it stored?

IMAGES: Use this section to leave a visual memory: a Photo, a Photocopy of a Pattern or Quilt Square. You could Draw an image, or use this space to attach Fabric Swatches. Use this page as you wish!

 # Handy Information

Yardage Inches

Yardage	Inches
1/8	4.5
1/4	9
1/3	12
1/2	18
2/3	24
3/4	27
1	36
1.5	54
2	72

Precut Sizes

Charm	5x5 in (42)
Fat 1/4	18x22 in (1)
Fat 1/8	9x22 in (1)
Jelly Roll	2.5x44 in (40)
Layer Cake	10x10 in (42)

Basic Bed and Quilt Sizes

Bed Size-	Mattress Size-	Quilt Size
Crib	27x52in	45x60in
Twin	40x75in	81x96in
Full	54x75in	72x90in
Queen	60x80in	90x108in
King	76x80 in	108x108in
Cal King	72x84in	104x110

Sewing and Quilting Acronyms ♡

PHD---Projects Half Done

UFO---Unfinished Object

STASH---Special Treasures All Secretly Hidden

TOAD---Trashed Object Abandoned in Disgust

TGIF---Thank God It's Finished

WOF---Width of Fabric

WIP---Work in Progress

FART---Fabric Acquisition Road Trip

FOB---Fear of Binding

OBW---One Block Wonder

VIP---Very Important Project

WISP- Work in Slow Progress

WOMBAT---Waste of Money, Batting and Time

WWIT---What Was I Thinking?

SNW---Stack And Whack

PIGS---Projects in Grocery Sacks

PP---Paper Piecing

NESTY- Not Even Started Yet

PFC---Professional Fabric Collector

SID---Stitch in Ditch

STABLE--- Stash Accumulation Beyond Life Expectancy

WAYWO---What Are You Working On?

TIH---There is Hope

FIU---Finish It Up

HSY---Haven't Started Yet

HST---Half Square Triangle

QIMM---Quilts In My Mind

SEX---Stash Enhancing Experience

Sew What

Project Index

Project Index

Project Details

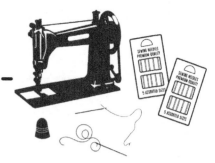

WHAT?
(Pattern Name/#, Quilt Name, Quilt Block, Description, Size, Garment, etc)

_____

_____

WHY?
(Special Occasion, Person or Just Because)

_____

WHEN?
(Dates of Start and Completion)

_____

HOW?
(Notes on Making this Project. Fabrics, Threads, Batting, Notions, etc.
Tips for Next time!)

_____

_____

_____

_____

WHERE?
(Where is this project now? Who has it?)

_____

Project Title:

Images
(Photo, Photocopy, Drawing, Fabric Swatches)

Project Details

WHAT?

(Pattern Name/#, Quilt Name, Quilt Block, Description, Size, Garment, etc)

_____

WHY?

(Special Occasion, Person or Just Because)

_____

WHEN?

(Dates of Start and Completion)

_____

HOW?

(Notes on Making this Project. Fabrics, Threads, Batting, Notions, etc.
Tips for Next time!)

_____

_____

_____

_____

WHERE?

(Where is this project now? Who has it?)

_____

Project Title:

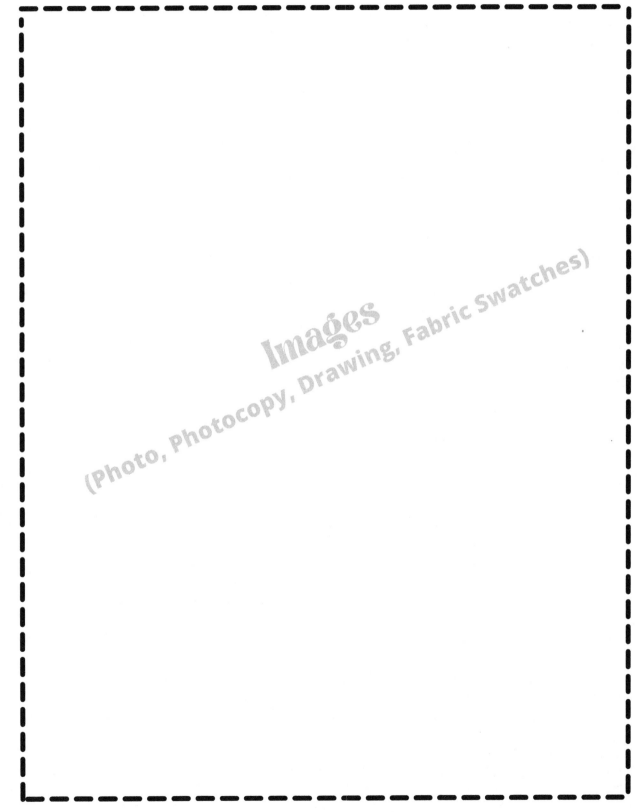

Images
(Photo, Photocopy, Drawing, Fabric Swatches)

Project Details

WHAT?

(Pattern Name/#, Quilt Name, Quilt Block, Description, Size, Garment, etc)

_____

_____

WHY?

(Special Occasion, Person or Just Because)

_____

WHEN?

(Dates of Start and Completion)

_____

HOW?

(Notes on Making this Project. Fabrics, Threads, Batting, Notions, etc.
Tips for Next time!)

_____

_____

_____

_____

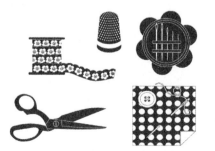

WHERE?

(Where is this project now? Who has it?)

_____

Project Title:

Images
(Photo, Photocopy, Drawing, Fabric Swatches)

Project Details

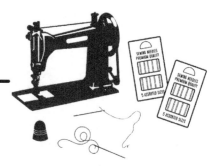

WHAT?

(Pattern Name /#, Quilt Name, Quilt Block, Description, Size, Garment, etc)

_____

_____

WHY?

(Special Occasion, Person or Just Because)

_____

WHEN?

(Dates of Start and Completion)

_____

HOW?

(Notes on Making this Project. Fabrics, Threads, Batting, Notions, etc.
Tips for Next time!)

_____

_____

_____

_____

WHERE?

(Where is this project now? Who has it?)

_____

Project Title:

Images
(Photo, Photocopy, Drawing, Fabric Swatches)

Project Details

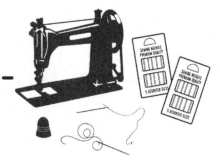

WHAT?
(Pattern Name /#, Quilt Name, Quilt Block, Description, Size, Garment, etc)

_____

_____

WHY?
(Special Occasion, Person or Just Because)

_____

WHEN?
(Dates of Start and Completion)

_____

HOW?
(Notes on Making this Project. Fabrics, Threads, Batting, Notions, etc.
Tips for Next time!)

_____

_____

_____

_____

WHERE?
(Where is this project now? Who has it?)

_____

Project Title:

Images
(Photo, Photocopy, Drawing, Fabric Swatches)

Project Details

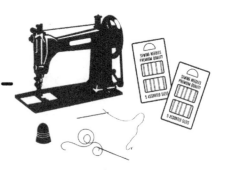

WHAT?
(Pattern Name /#, Quilt Name, Quilt Block, Description, Size, Garment, etc)

_____

_____

WHY?
(Special Occasion, Person or Just Because)

_____

WHEN?
(Dates of Start and Completion)

_____

HOW?
(Notes on Making this Project. Fabrics, Threads, Batting, Notions, etc.
Tips for Next time!)

_____

_____

_____

_____

WHERE?
(Where is this project now? Who has it?)

_____

Project Title:

Images
(Photo, Photocopy, Drawing, Fabric Swatches)

Project Details

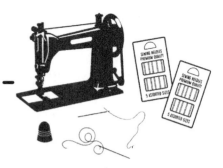

WHAT?
(Pattern Name /#, Quilt Name, Quilt Block, Description, Size, Garment, etc)

_____

_____

WHY?
(Special Occasion, Person or Just Because)

_____

WHEN?
(Dates of Start and Completion)

_____

HOW?
(Notes on Making this Project. Fabrics, Threads, Batting, Notions, etc.
Tips for Next time!)

_____

_____

_____

_____

WHERE?
(Where is this project now? Who has it?)

_____

Project Title:

Images
(Photo, Photocopy, Drawing, Fabric Swatches)

Project Details

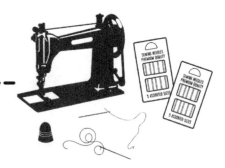

WHAT?

(Pattern Name /#, Quilt Name, Quilt Block, Description, Size, Garment, etc)

_____

_____

WHY?

(Special Occasion, Person or Just Because)

_____

WHEN?

(Dates of Start and Completion)

_____

HOW?

(Notes on Making this Project. Fabrics, Threads, Batting, Notions, etc.
Tips for Next time!)

_____

_____

_____

_____

WHERE?

(Where is this project now? Who has it?)

_____

Project Title:

Project Details

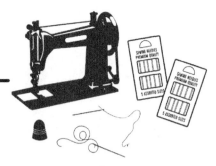

WHAT?

(Pattern Name /#, Quilt Name, Quilt Block, Description, Size, Garment, etc)

_____

_____

WHY?

(Special Occasion, Person or Just Because)

_____

WHEN?

(Dates of Start and Completion)

_____

HOW?

(Notes on Making this Project. Fabrics, Threads, Batting, Notions, etc.
Tips for Next time!)

_____

_____

_____

_____

_____

WHERE?

(Where is this project now? Who has it?)

_____

Project Title:

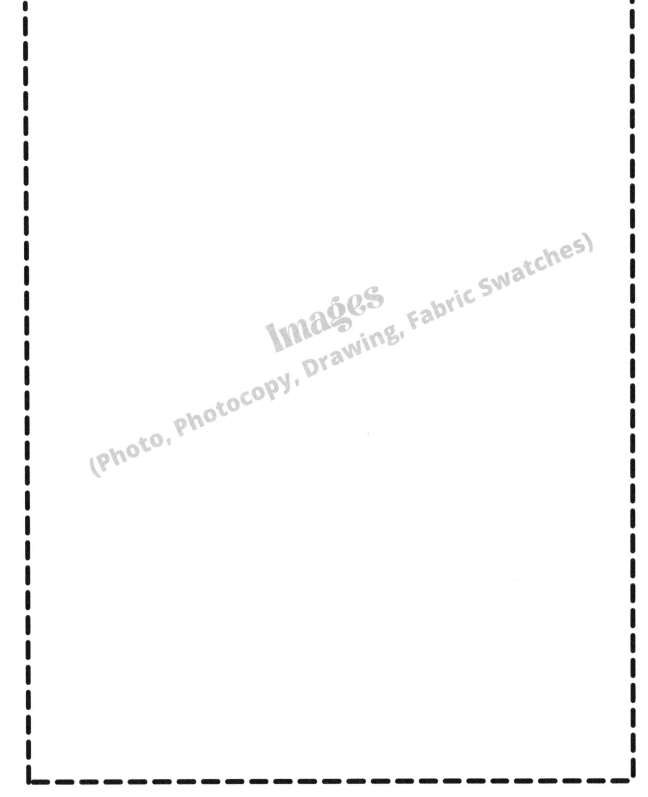

Project Details

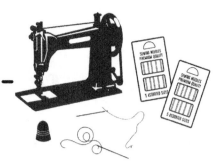

WHAT?

(Pattern Name /#, Quilt Name, Quilt Block, Description, Size, Garment, etc)

_____

_____

WHY?

(Special Occasion, Person or Just Because)

_____

WHEN?

(Dates of Start and Completion)

_____

HOW?

(Notes on Making this Project. Fabrics, Threads, Batting, Notions, etc.
Tips for Next time!)

_____

_____

_____

_____

_____

WHERE?

(Where is this project now? Who has it?)

_____

Project Title:

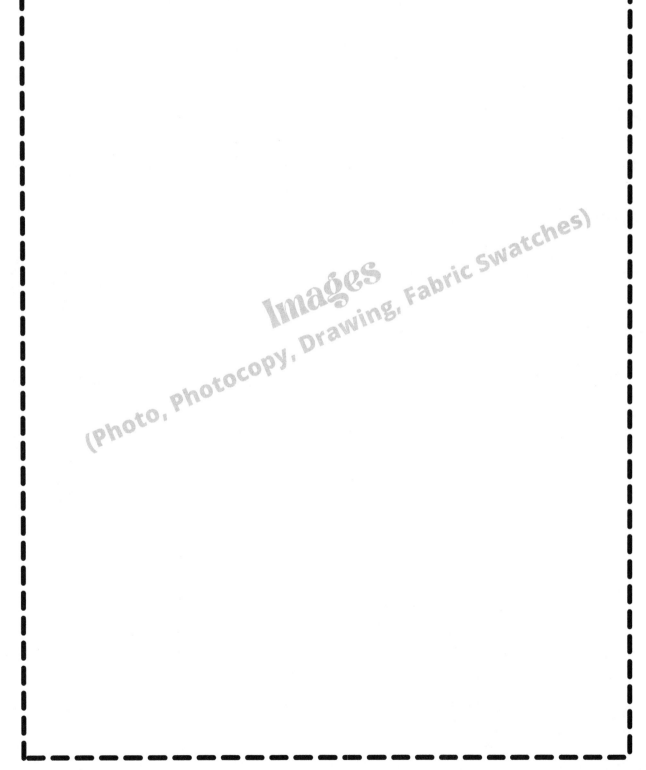

Images
(Photo, Photocopy, Drawing, Fabric Swatches)

Project Details

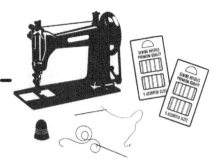

WHAT?
(Pattern Name /#, Quilt Name, Quilt Block, Description, Size, Garment, etc)

_____

_____

WHY?
(Special Occasion, Person or Just Because)

_____

WHEN?
(Dates of Start and Completion)

_____

HOW?
(Notes on Making this Project. Fabrics, Threads, Batting, Notions, etc.
Tips for Next time!)

_____

_____

_____

_____

WHERE?
(Where is this project now? Who has it?)

_____

Project Title:

Images
(Photo, Photocopy, Drawing, Fabric Swatches)

Project Details

WHAT?

(Pattern Name /#, Quilt Name, Quilt Block, Description, Size, Garment, etc)

_____

_____

WHY?

(Special Occasion, Person or Just Because)

_____

WHEN?

(Dates of Start and Completion)

_____

HOW?

(Notes on Making this Project. Fabrics, Threads, Batting, Notions, etc.
Tips for Next time!)

_____

_____

_____

_____

WHERE?

(Where is this project now? Who has it?)

_____

Project Title:

Images
(Photo, Photocopy, Drawing, Fabric Swatches)

Project Details

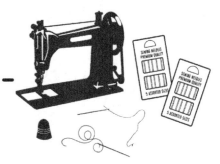

WHAT?

(Pattern Name /#, Quilt Name, Quilt Block, Description, Size, Garment, etc)

_____

WHY?

(Special Occasion, Person or Just Because)

_____

WHEN?

(Dates of Start and Completion)

_____

HOW?

(Notes on Making this Project. Fabrics, Threads, Batting, Notions, etc.
Tips for Next time!)

_____

_____

_____

_____

WHERE?

(Where is this project now? Who has it?)

_____

Project Title:

Images
(Photo, Photocopy, Drawing, Fabric Swatches)

Project Details

WHAT?

(Pattern Name /#, Quilt Name, Quilt Block, Description, Size, Garment, etc)

_____

WHY?

(Special Occasion, Person or Just Because)

_____

WHEN?

(Dates of Start and Completion)

_____

HOW?

(Notes on Making this Project. Fabrics, Threads, Batting, Notions, etc.
Tips for Next time!)

_____

_____

_____

_____

WHERE?

(Where is this project now? Who has it?)

_____

Project Title:

Project Details

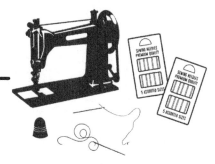

WHAT?
(Pattern Name /#, Quilt Name, Quilt Block, Description, Size, Garment, etc)

_____

WHY?
(Special Occasion, Person or Just Because)

_____

WHEN?

(Dates of Start and Completion)

_____

HOW?

(Notes on Making this Project. Fabrics, Threads, Batting, Notions, etc.
Tips for Next time!)

_____

_____

_____

_____

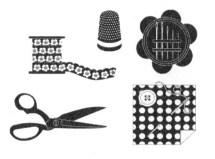

WHERE?

(Where is this project now? Who has it?)

_____

Project Title:

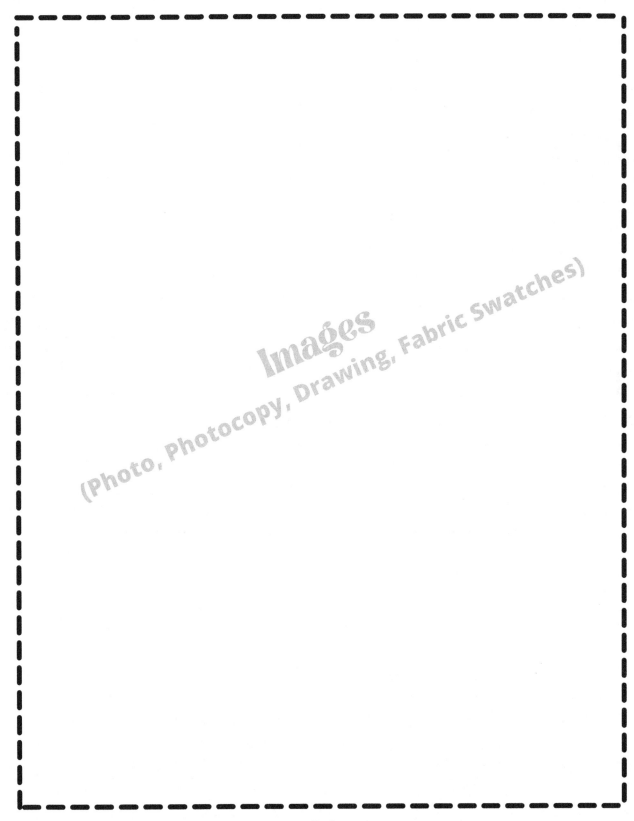

Project Details

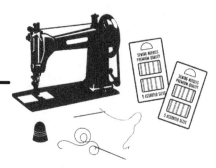

WHAT?

(Pattern Name /#, Quilt Name, Quilt Block, Description, Size, Garment, etc)

_____

WHY?

(Special Occasion, Person or Just Because)

_____

WHEN?

(Dates of Start and Completion)

_____

HOW?

(Notes on Making this Project. Fabrics, Threads, Batting, Notions, etc.
Tips for Next time!)

_____

_____

_____

_____

WHERE?

(Where is this project now? Who has it?)

_____

Project Title:

Images
(Photo, Photocopy, Drawing, Fabric Swatches)

Project Details

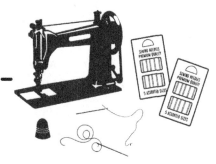

WHAT?

(Pattern Name /#, Quilt Name, Quilt Block, Description, Size, Garment, etc)

_____

_____

WHY?

(Special Occasion, Person or Just Because)

_____

WHEN?

(Dates of Start and Completion)

_____

HOW?

(Notes on Making this Project. Fabrics, Threads, Batting, Notions, etc.
Tips for Next time!)

_____

_____

_____

_____

_____

WHERE?

(Where is this project now? Who has it?)

_____

Project Title:

Images
(Photo, Photocopy, Drawing, Fabric Swatches)

Project Details

WHAT?

(Pattern Name /#, Quilt Name, Quilt Block, Description, Size, Garment, etc)

_____

_____

WHY?

(Special Occasion, Person or Just Because)

_____

WHEN?

(Dates of Start and Completion)

_____

HOW?

(Notes on Making this Project. Fabrics, Threads, Batting, Notions, etc.
Tips for Next time!)

_____

_____

_____

_____

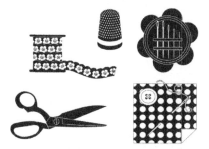

WHERE?

(Where is this project now? Who has it?)

_____

Project Title:

Images
(Photo, Photocopy, Drawing, Fabric Swatches)

Project Details

WHAT?

(Pattern Name /#, Quilt Name, Quilt Block, Description, Size, Garment, etc)

_____

_____

WHY?

(Special Occasion, Person or Just Because)

_____

WHEN?

(Dates of Start and Completion)

_____

HOW?

(Notes on Making this Project. Fabrics, Threads, Batting, Notions, etc.
Tips for Next time!)

_____

_____

_____

_____

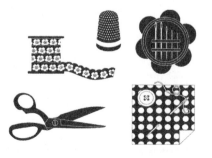

WHERE?

(Where is this project now? Who has it?)

_____

Project Title:

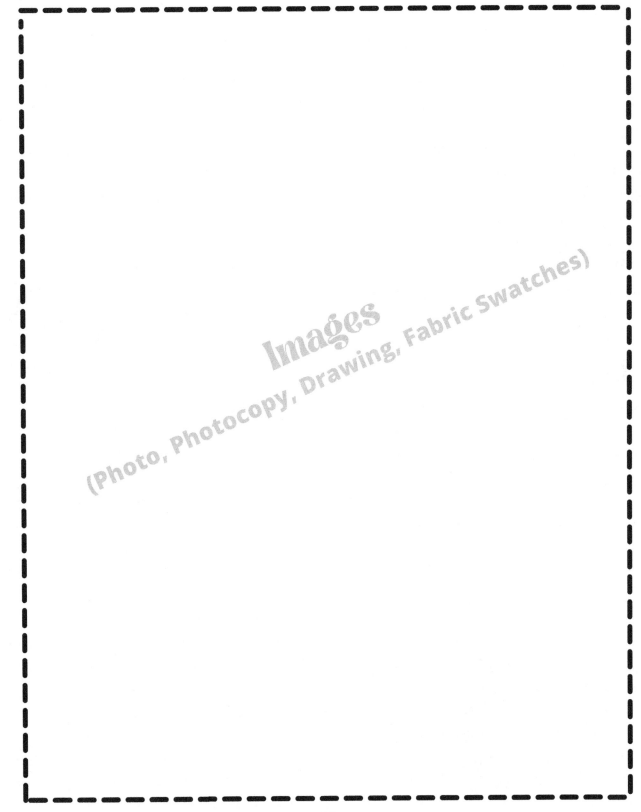

Images
(Photo, Photocopy, Drawing, Fabric Swatches)

Project Details

WHAT?

(Pattern Name /#, Quilt Name, Quilt Block, Description, Size, Garment, etc)

_____

_____

WHY?

(Special Occasion, Person or Just Because)

_____

WHEN?

(Dates of Start and Completion)

_____

HOW?

(Notes on Making this Project. Fabrics, Threads, Batting, Notions, etc.
Tips for Next time!)

_____

_____

_____

_____

WHERE?

(Where is this project now? Who has it?)

_____

Project Title:

Project Details

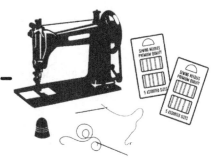

WHAT?
(Pattern Name /#, Quilt Name, Quilt Block, Description, Size, Garment, etc)

_____

_____

WHY?
(Special Occasion, Person or Just Because)

_____

WHEN?
(Dates of Start and Completion)

_____

HOW?
(Notes on Making this Project. Fabrics, Threads, Batting, Notions, etc.
Tips for Next time!)

_____

_____

_____

_____

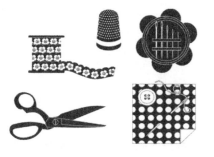

WHERE?
(Where is this project now? Who has it?)

_____

Project Title:

Project Details

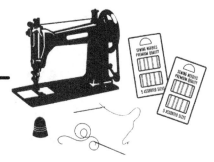

WHAT?
(Pattern Name /#, Quilt Name, Quilt Block, Description, Size, Garment, etc)

_____

WHY?
(Special Occasion, Person or Just Because)

_____

WHEN?

(Dates of Start and Completion)

_____

HOW?

(Notes on Making this Project. Fabrics, Threads, Batting, Notions, etc.
Tips for Next time!)

_____

_____

_____

_____

WHERE?

(Where is this project now? Who has it?)

_____

Project Title:

Images
(Photo, Photocopy, Drawing, Fabric Swatches)

Project Details

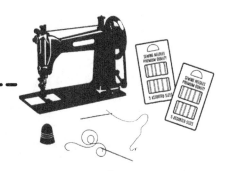

WHAT?

(Pattern Name /#, Quilt Name, Quilt Block, Description, Size, Garment, etc)

_____

_____

WHY?

(Special Occasion, Person or Just Because)

_____

WHEN?

(Dates of Start and Completion)

_____

HOW?

(Notes on Making this Project. Fabrics, Threads, Batting, Notions, etc.
Tips for Next time!)

_____

_____

_____

_____

WHERE?

(Where is this project now? Who has it?)

_____

Project Title:

Images
(Photo, Photocopy, Drawing, Fabric Swatches)

Project Details

WHAT?

(Pattern Name /#, Quilt Name, Quilt Block, Description, Size, Garment, etc)

_____

WHY?

(Special Occasion, Person or Just Because)

_____

WHEN?

(Dates of Start and Completion)

_____

HOW?

(Notes on Making this Project. Fabrics, Threads, Batting, Notions, etc.
Tips for Next time!)

_____

_____

_____

_____

WHERE?

(Where is this project now? Who has it?)

_____

Project Title:

Images
(Photo, Photocopy, Drawing, Fabric Swatches)

Project Details

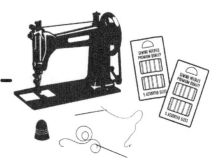

WHAT?
(Pattern Name /#, Quilt Name, Quilt Block, Description, Size, Garment, etc)

_____

_____

WHY?
(Special Occasion, Person or Just Because)

_____

WHEN?

(Dates of Start and Completion)

_____

HOW?

(Notes on Making this Project. Fabrics, Threads, Batting, Notions, etc.
Tips for Next time!)

_____

_____

_____

_____

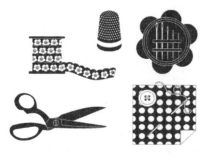

WHERE?
(Where is this project now? Who has it?)

_____

Project Title:

Images
(Photo, Photocopy, Drawing, Fabric Swatches)

Project Details

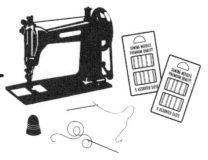

WHAT?
(Pattern Name /#, Quilt Name, Quilt Block, Description, Size, Garment, etc)

_____

_____

WHY?
(Special Occasion, Person or Just Because)

_____

WHEN?
(Dates of Start and Completion)

_____

HOW?
(Notes on Making this Project. Fabrics, Threads, Batting, Notions, etc.
Tips for Next time!)

_____

_____

_____

_____

WHERE?
(Where is this project now? Who has it?)

_____

Project Title:

Images
(Photo, Photocopy, Drawing, Fabric Swatches)

Project Details

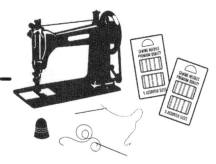

WHAT?
(Pattern Name /#, Quilt Name, Quilt Block, Description, Size, Garment, etc)

_____

_____

WHY?
(Special Occasion, Person or Just Because)

_____

WHEN?
(Dates of Start and Completion)

_____

HOW?
(Notes on Making this Project. Fabrics, Threads, Batting, Notions, etc.
Tips for Next time!)

_____

_____

_____

_____

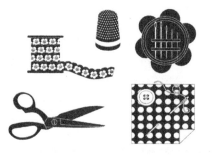

WHERE?
(Where is this project now? Who has it?)

_____

Project Title:

Images
(Photo, Photocopy, Drawing, Fabric Swatches)

Project Details

WHAT?

(Pattern Name /#, Quilt Name, Quilt Block, Description, Size, Garment, etc)

_____

_____

WHY?

(Special Occasion, Person or Just Because)

_____

WHEN?

(Dates of Start and Completion)

_____

HOW?

(Notes on Making this Project. Fabrics, Threads, Batting, Notions, etc.
Tips for Next time!)

_____

_____

_____

_____

WHERE?

(Where is this project now? Who has it?)

_____

Project Title:

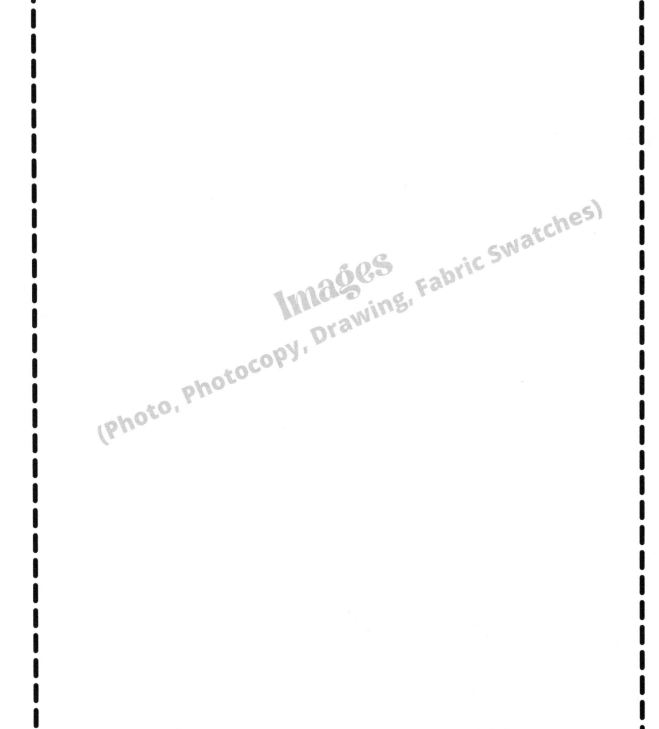

Project Details

WHAT?
(Pattern Name /#, Quilt Name, Quilt Block, Description, Size, Garment, etc)

_____

_____

WHY?
(Special Occasion, Person or Just Because)

_____

WHEN?
(Dates of Start and Completion)

_____

HOW?
(Notes on Making this Project. Fabrics, Threads, Batting, Notions, etc.
Tips for Next time!)

_____

_____

_____

_____

WHERE?
(Where is this project now? Who has it?)

_____

Project Title:

Images
(Photo, Photocopy, Drawing, Fabric Swatches)

Project Details

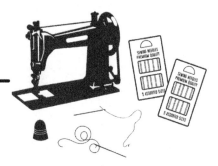

WHAT?

(Pattern Name /#, Quilt Name, Quilt Block, Description, Size, Garment, etc)

_____

_____

WHY?

(Special Occasion, Person or Just Because)

_____

WHEN?

(Dates of Start and Completion)

_____

HOW?

(Notes on Making this Project. Fabrics, Threads, Batting, Notions, etc.
Tips for Next time!)

_____

_____

_____

_____

WHERE?

(Where is this project now? Who has it?)

_____

Project Title:

Project Details

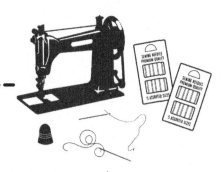

WHAT?

(Pattern Name /#, Quilt Name, Quilt Block, Description, Size, Garment, etc)

_____

WHY?

(Special Occasion, Person or Just Because)

_____

WHEN?

(Dates of Start and Completion)

_____

HOW?

(Notes on Making this Project. Fabrics, Threads, Batting, Notions, etc.
Tips for Next time!)

_____

_____

_____

_____

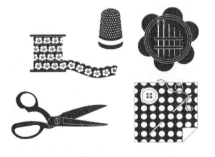

WHERE?

(Where is this project now? Who has it?)

_____

Project Title:

Images
(Photo, Photocopy, Drawing, Fabric Swatches)

Project Details

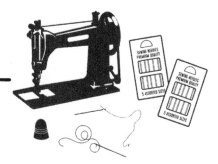

WHAT?

(Pattern Name /#, Quilt Name, Quilt Block, Description, Size, Garment, etc)

_____

WHY?

(Special Occasion, Person or Just Because)

_____

WHEN?

(Dates of Start and Completion)

_____

HOW?

(Notes on Making this Project. Fabrics, Threads, Batting, Notions, etc.
Tips for Next time!)

_____

_____

_____

_____

WHERE?

(Where is this project now? Who has it?)

_____

Project Title:

Images
(Photo, Photocopy, Drawing, Fabric Swatches)

Project Details

WHAT?

(Pattern Name /#, Quilt Name, Quilt Block, Description, Size, Garment, etc)

_____

WHY?

(Special Occasion, Person or Just Because)

_____

WHEN?

(Dates of Start and Completion)

_____

HOW?

(Notes on Making this Project. Fabrics, Threads, Batting, Notions, etc.
Tips for Next time!)

_____

_____

_____

_____

WHERE?

(Where is this project now? Who has it?)

_____

70

Project Title:

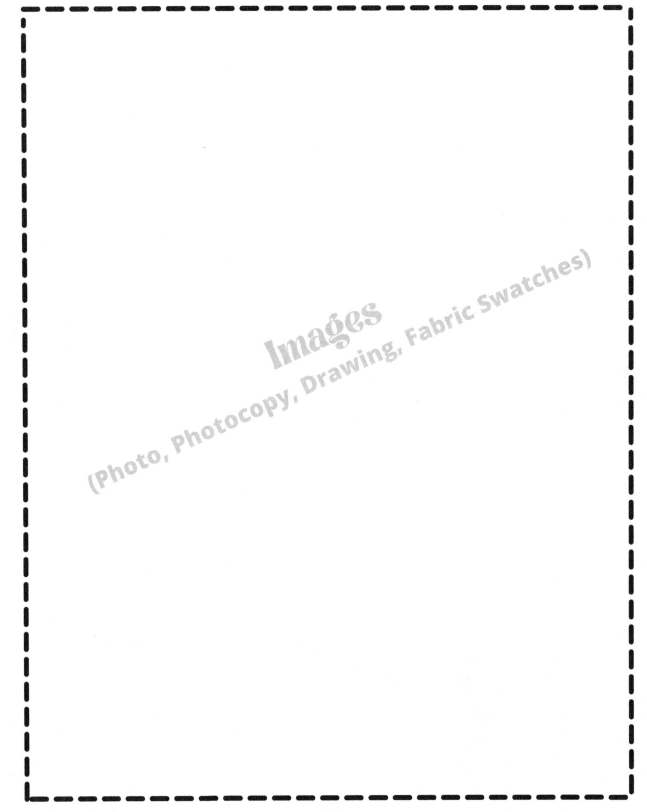

Images
(Photo, Photocopy, Drawing, Fabric Swatches)

Project Details

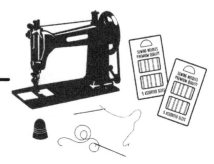

WHAT?

(Pattern Name /#, Quilt Name, Quilt Block, Description, Size, Garment, etc)

_____

_____

WHY?

(Special Occasion, Person or Just Because)

_____

WHEN?

(Dates of Start and Completion)

_____

HOW?

(Notes on Making this Project. Fabrics, Threads, Batting, Notions, etc.
Tips for Next time!)

_____

_____

_____

_____

WHERE?

(Where is this project now? Who has it?)

_____

Project Title:

Images
(Photo, Photocopy, Drawing, Fabric Swatches)

Project Details

WHAT?

(Pattern Name /#, Quilt Name, Quilt Block, Description, Size, Garment, etc)

_____

_____

WHY?

(Special Occasion, Person or Just Because)

_____

WHEN?

(Dates of Start and Completion)

_____

HOW?

(Notes on Making this Project. Fabrics, Threads, Batting, Notions, etc.
Tips for Next time!)

_____

_____

_____

_____

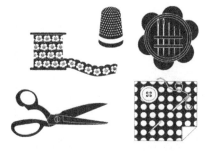

WHERE?

(Where is this project now? Who has it?)

_____

Project Title:

Images
(Photo, Photocopy, Drawing, Fabric Swatches)

Project Details

WHAT?
(Pattern Name /#, Quilt Name, Quilt Block, Description, Size, Garment, etc)

_____

WHY?
(Special Occasion, Person or Just Because)

_____

WHEN?
(Dates of Start and Completion)

_____

HOW?
(Notes on Making this Project. Fabrics, Threads, Batting, Notions, etc.
Tips for Next time!)

_____

_____

_____

_____

WHERE?
(Where is this project now? Who has it?)

_____

Project Title:

Project Details

WHAT?

(Pattern Name /#, Quilt Name, Quilt Block, Description, Size, Garment, etc)

_____

_____

WHY?

(Special Occasion, Person or Just Because)

_____

WHEN?

(Dates of Start and Completion)

_____

HOW?

(Notes on Making this Project. Fabrics, Threads, Batting, Notions, etc.
Tips for Next time!)

_____

_____

_____

_____

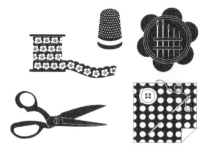

WHERE?

(Where is this project now? Who has it?)

_____

Project Title:

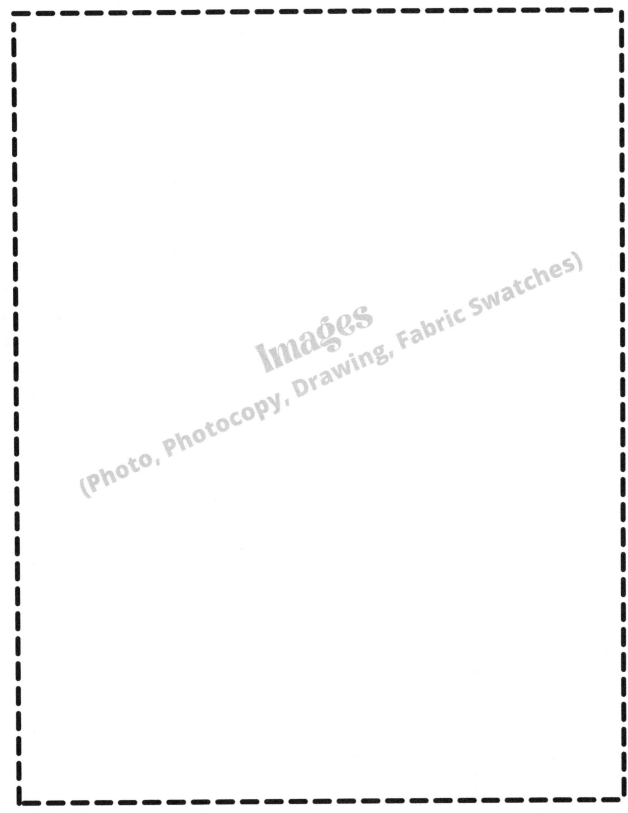

Images
(Photo, Photocopy, Drawing, Fabric Swatches)

Project Details

WHAT?

(Pattern Name /#, Quilt Name, Quilt Block, Description, Size, Garment, etc)

_____

_____

WHY?

(Special Occasion, Person or Just Because)

_____

WHEN?

(Dates of Start and Completion)

_____

HOW?

(Notes on Making this Project. Fabrics, Threads, Batting, Notions, etc.
Tips for Next time!)

_____

_____

_____

_____

WHERE?

(Where is this project now? Who has it?)

_____

80

Project Title:

Images
(Photo, Photocopy, Drawing, Fabric Swatches)

Project Details

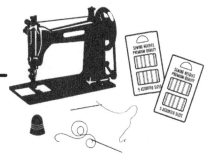

WHAT?

(Pattern Name /#, Quilt Name, Quilt Block, Description, Size, Garment, etc)

_____

_____

WHY?

(Special Occasion, Person or Just Because)

_____

WHEN?

(Dates of Start and Completion)

_____

HOW?

(Notes on Making this Project. Fabrics, Threads, Batting, Notions, etc.
Tips for Next time!)

_____

_____

_____

_____

WHERE?

(Where is this project now? Who has it?)

_____

Project Title:

Images

(Photo, Photocopy, Drawing, Fabric Swatches)

Project Details

WHAT?

(Pattern Name /#, Quilt Name, Quilt Block, Description, Size, Garment, etc)

_____

_____

WHY?

(Special Occasion, Person or Just Because)

_____

WHEN?

(Dates of Start and Completion)

_____

HOW?

(Notes on Making this Project. Fabrics, Threads, Batting, Notions, etc.
Tips for Next time!)

_____

_____

_____

_____

WHERE?

(Where is this project now? Who has it?)

_____

Project Title:

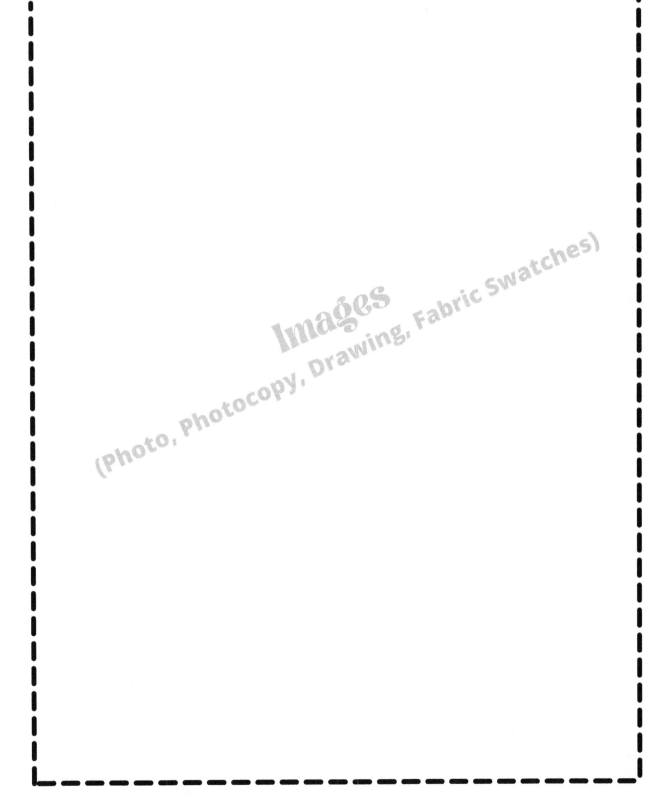

Images
(Photo, Photocopy, Drawing, Fabric Swatches)

Project Details

WHAT?

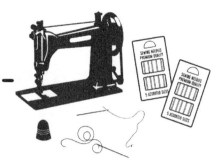

(Pattern Name /#, Quilt Name, Quilt Block, Description, Size, Garment, etc)

_____

_____

WHY?

(Special Occasion, Person or Just Because)

_____

WHEN?

(Dates of Start and Completion)

_____

HOW?

(Notes on Making this Project. Fabrics, Threads, Batting, Notions, etc.
Tips for Next time!)

_____

_____

_____

_____

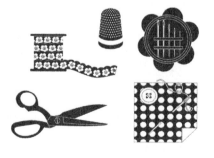

WHERE?

(Where is this project now? Who has it?)

_____

Project Title:

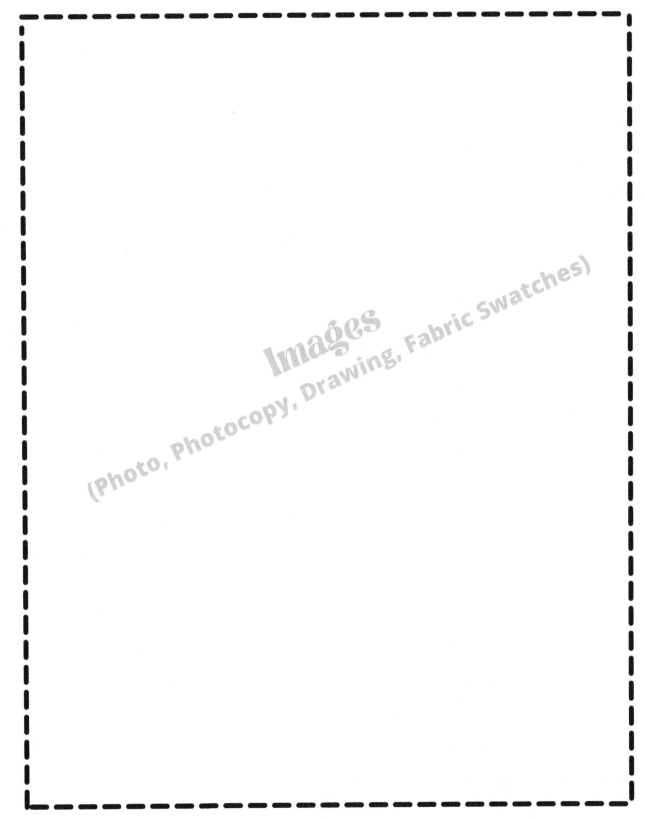

Images
(Photo, Photocopy, Drawing, Fabric Swatches)

Project Details

WHAT?
(Pattern Name /#, Quilt Name, Quilt Block, Description, Size, Garment, etc)

_____

_____

WHY?
(Special Occasion, Person or Just Because)

_____

WHEN?

(Dates of Start and Completion)

_____

HOW?

(Notes on Making this Project. Fabrics, Threads, Batting, Notions, etc.
Tips for Next time!)

_____

_____

_____

_____

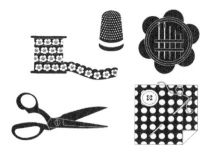

WHERE?
(Where is this project now? Who has it?)

_____

Project Title:

Project Details

WHAT?

(Pattern Name /#, Quilt Name, Quilt Block, Description, Size, Garment, etc)

_____

WHY?

(Special Occasion, Person or Just Because)

_____

WHEN?

(Dates of Start and Completion)

_____

HOW?

(Notes on Making this Project. Fabrics, Threads, Batting, Notions, etc.
Tips for Next time!)

_____

_____

_____

_____

WHERE?

(Where is this project now? Who has it?)

_____

Project Title:

Images
(Photo, Photocopy, Drawing, Fabric Swatches)

Project Details

WHAT?

(Pattern Name /#, Quilt Name, Quilt Block, Description, Size, Garment, etc)

_____

_____

WHY?

(Special Occasion, Person or Just Because)

_____

WHEN?

(Dates of Start and Completion)

_____

HOW?

(Notes on Making this Project. Fabrics, Threads, Batting, Notions, etc.
Tips for Next time!)

_____

_____

_____

_____

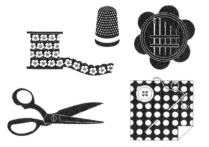

WHERE?

(Where is this project now? Who has it?)

_____

Project Title:

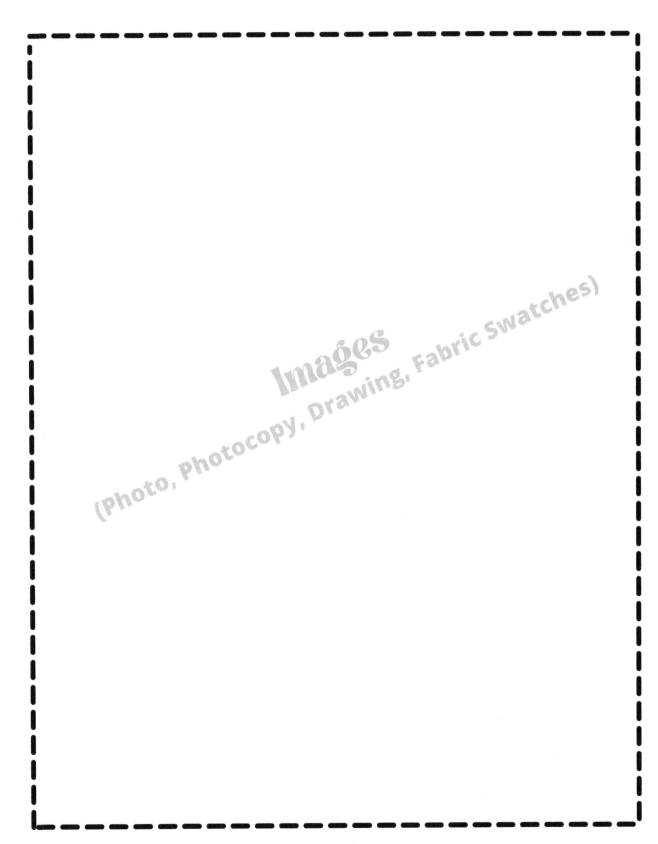

Project Details

WHAT?

(Pattern Name /#, Quilt Name, Quilt Block, Description, Size, Garment, etc)

_____

_____

WHY?

(Special Occasion, Person or Just Because)

_____

WHEN?

(Dates of Start and Completion)

_____

HOW?

(Notes on Making this Project. Fabrics, Threads, Batting, Notions, etc.
Tips for Next time!)

_____

_____

_____

_____

WHERE?

(Where is this project now? Who has it?)

_____

Project Title:

Images
(Photo, Photocopy, Drawing, Fabric Swatches)

Project Details

WHAT?

(Pattern Name /#, Quilt Name, Quilt Block, Description, Size, Garment, etc)

_____

WHY?

(Special Occasion, Person or Just Because)

_____

WHEN?

(Dates of Start and Completion)

_____

HOW?

(Notes on Making this Project. Fabrics, Threads, Batting, Notions, etc.
Tips for Next time!)

_____

_____

_____

_____

WHERE?

(Where is this project now? Who has it?)

_____

Project Title:

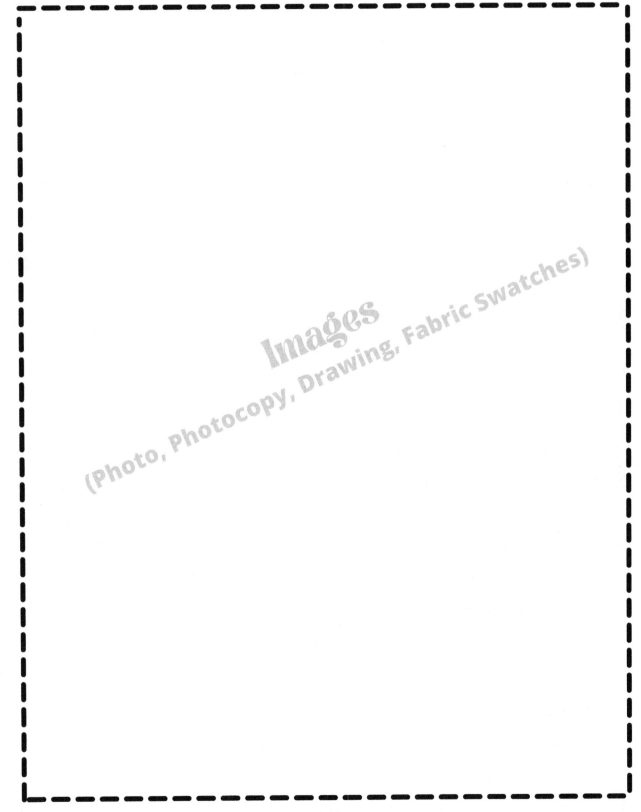

Images
(Photo, Photocopy, Drawing, Fabric Swatches)

Dedication

Dedicated to the Wonderful and Inspiring
Members of the Lakewood Sewing Circle

Printed in Great Britain
by Amazon

45650207R00057